BEYOND THE FRONT DOOR

Cultivating Rhythms of Abiding in Jesus

written by

ELIZABETH GIGER

Made Sacred Creations | Bloomington, IL

Copyright © 2021 by Elizabeth Giger

All rights reserved. No part of this book may be reproduced or used in any manner without written permission of the copyright owner except for the use of quotations in a book review. For more information, contact: elizabeth@madesacred.com

FIRST EDITION

Unless otherwise indicated, all Scripture quotations are from The ESV® Bible (The Holy Bible, English Standard Version®), copyright © 2001 by Crossway, a publishing ministry of Good News Publishers. Used by permission. All rights reserved.

Scripture quotations marked (NIV) are taken from the Holy Bible, New International Version®, NIV®. Copyright © 1973, 1978, 1984, 2011 by Biblica, Inc.™ Used by permission of Zondervan. All rights reserved worldwide. www.zondervan.com The "NIV" and "New International Version" are trademarks registered in the United States Patent and Trademark Office by Biblica, Inc™

*Book design and original cover art
by Thumbprint Creative Arts*

ISBN: 979-8-7012-4140-2

www.madesacred.com

As the Father has loved me,

so have I loved you.

Abide in my love.

John 15:9

this book is dedicated

to my Mama and Daddy — you have been my support and encouragement all along. thank you for loving me so well.

to Daniel — this book would not exist if not for your expert child-wrangling. thank you for believing in me.

Contents

Chapter One
Introduction: Discovering Home 1

Chapter Two
You are Here (But Why?) 7

Chapter Three
Abiding in the Wait: "My Thirst is Rising" 17

Chapter Four
Lectio Divina: Drink Deeply 29

Chapter Five
The Cure for the Sickness of Busy 39

Chapter Six
Finding the Holy and Hidden Heart of our Daily Routine 47

Chapter Seven
Abiding in Suffering: Refuge in the Storm 57

Chapter Eight
Seeing God in the Small and the Slow 67

Chapter Nine
Giving God Stillness and Space to Do His Good Work 77

Chapter Ten
Conclusion: Coming Home to Stay 85

Further Resources 90

Endnotes 91

Bibliography 96

Author Bio 98

Acknowledgements

Thank you to all the faithful readers of my blog, Made Sacred (madesacred.com). You have allowed me to experiment with my words for more than nine years now. I have honed my craft on your listening ears, and I am grateful.

Thank you to my editor, Joan Sherman, and book designer, Kristi Griffith, for making this book more beautiful than I could have made it on my own.

Thank you to all who patiently read my first drafts, helping me to polish and craft my words. Dr. J.K. Jones, Deb Knoles (my second mama!), Amanda Wen, Todd Daly, Deb Alexander, Auntie Mary Ann, Jill Warren, Devon Stribling — this would be a lesser book without you.

Thank you to my parents. You have made it easier to love God by the way that you love me. You have always been my greatest encouragers. Daddy, your comments on so many of my blog posts pulled me out of a my-writing-will-never-be-any-good funk. Mama, you saved my title dilemma!

Thank you to my girls. It is my greatest privilege to be your mother, to be allowed to shepherd your hearts through these growing-up years. My writing will always be relegated to the cracks of my time, and you shall have my best while you are young.

Thank you to my Daniel. You have always believed in me and what God was doing through me, even more than I believed in it myself. Thank you for the hours of writing time you gave me by taking care of the girls on your own every Wednesday evening after a long day of work. I see you and I am so grateful for you.

Most of all — to you, Abba. The gift of waking up to your presence is a gift beyond measure. Soli Deo gloria.

CHAPTER ONE

Introduction

Discovering Home

We are to make Jesus our home. We are to make him the place where we live out our ordinary, everyday lives and the place where we dwell in times of great storms. We are to make him the place we remain every moment of every day.

CHAPTER ONE

Introduction — Discovering Home

Abide in me, and I in you.
John 15:4

Christmas in Germany is breathtaking. Every little scenic village you stumble upon, it seems, is decorated to the hilt. White starlight twinkles on each centuries-old building. Snow dusts every cobblestone street. The scent of freshly baked bread seeps into your soul. Everywhere you look, you find enchantment. Yet to a twenty-one-year-old college student nearing the end of her semester abroad, no matter how idyllic the scene, I still felt an ache, a tug, a touch of cold, deep down inside.

As a junior in college, I received the gift of studying in Greece from my parents and grandparents. During the semester, I traveled to ancient places: Athens, Israel, the seven churches in Turkey. I spent the last two weeks of my semester experiencing the glories of Europe. I savored every moment.

And I missed home.

I was a traveler — a pilgrim, in Biblical language — and whether gazing at the snow-capped Swiss Alps or walking the shore of the Sea of Galilee, my heart was pulling me away from these places toward home.

The day came for me to head back to the States. Home. That tug I had mostly resisted all semester grew stronger. Two flights, one volcano (around whose ash we had to detour), and one wild dash through an airport later, I was in the arms of my parents. It wasn't my house — we were in the middle of a busy airport — yet that cold, deep inside, had melted into warmth. If I had ever doubted that home was where Mom and Dad were, that moment anchored the two together immutably. It did not particularly matter the place or the circumstances; if I was with my parents, I was home.

Home. Where you live, dwell, abide. Most often, home involves *people* even more than a place. Your people. The people with whom you are safe and joyful and comforted. The people with whom you live your mundane kind of life as well as those to whom you cling when trouble comes. Even for those who have never experienced this caliber of home, this ideal still powerfully draws the heart. Home.

Jesus tells us that we must abide in him in order to bear fruit, in order to be transformed into his likeness.[1] That word, *abide*, is such a rich word, containing the ideas of peace, comfort, fulfilled needs, knowing and being known, constancy, and close relationships. In short, all that is true, good, and beautiful. Home.

In his gospel, John writes of Jesus using the word *abide* repeatedly during his last night with his disciples. Jesus spoke of abiding in him and in his love, of allowing his words to abide in us, of abiding in him the way a branch abides in a vine. Remaining attached at all times and in all seasons, unable to produce fruit on its own but having to rely on the vine to do the work of sustaining life, submitting to whatever the vinedresser does and trusting that what he is doing will produce the most abundant fruit — there is a reason Jesus chose this particular image.[2] I imagine that as he was speaking, the apostles saw in a sudden blaze the image of Jesus, just a few hours earlier, holding up a cup of the fruit of the vine. *Drink it, all of you, for this is my blood of the covenant, which is poured out for many for the forgiveness of sins.*[3]

What does this mean? What in the world, what in this crazy, busy, distracting world does it mean to abide in Jesus? Among other things, we abide in Jesus by spending time gazing at him through the twin disciplines of silence and solitude, and we allow Jesus' words to abide in us through the discipline of *lectio divina*, practices about which I will write more in later chapters.

If we do this work of abiding, Jesus promises, then the Father will be glorified and we will bear much fruit.[4] Fruit that, among other things, allows us to love one another in the same way that Jesus loves us.

We are, in other words, to make Jesus our home. We are to make him the place where we live out our ordinary, everyday lives and the place where we dwell in times of great storms. We are to make him the place we remain every moment of every day. Weaving these holy habits of silence, solitude, and *lectio divina* into our lives softens our hearts and awakens our minds to the presence and workings of God all around us. Dwelling in God allows the compassion of God to flow through us into the lives of others. Nineteenth century author A. W. Tozer wrote, "God wills that we should push on into His Presence and live our whole life there."[5] These disciplines allow us to do just this.

Scripture is full of the idea that the life we live on this earth is fleeting. We are temporary travelers. King David speaks of us being sojourners, that there is no abiding here in this life.[6] Peter, who heard Jesus' message of abiding in him as the branches abide in the vine, also wrote that we are sojourners and exiles.[7] This world is not our home and never can be.

Jesus is.

Jesus promised that he would never leave us,[8] but we are creatures who lean into our physicality more than our spirituality and are mostly unaware of his presence with us. So many days I struggle to believe this promise ... days in which I hurl harsh words at my precious children rather than trusting in God's way of gentleness. Days in which I aim subtle gestures and tones of coldness toward my husband rather than trusting in God's way of love. Days in which I am so caught up in my own desires and needs that I turn my back on those I love most rather than trusting in God's promise to give me all I need.

Spiritual disciplines help us wake up to the ways in which Jesus fulfills His promise to always be with us. The more we practice these habits, the more we are filled up with God and are able to spill out his love and compassion into those around us. The more we practice these disciplines, the more we move ourselves into a place where the Holy Spirit can work to transform us to look like Jesus. The more we weave these practices into our everyday lives, the more we are making Jesus our home.

To be filled up with God. To be awake to his presence every moment. To be still and know him in the same way that we are known, although we will not reach perfection of knowing until we see God face to face. God is perfect and we are most definitely not, yet he knows us and loves us regardless. Most remarkably of all, God desires for us to know and love him in the same way. This is what we are desperate for in this chaotic world: an inner peace and joy that remains in us as we begin to look more like Jesus. This is what God promises us as we learn to abide in him.[9]

"Come, my brethren, and let us day by day set ourselves at His feet, and meditate on this word of His, with an eye fixed on Him alone. Let us set ourselves in quiet trust before Him, waiting to hear His holy voice — the still small voice that is mightier than the storm that rends the rocks — breathing its quickening spirit within us, as He speaks: 'Abide in me.'"[10]

CHAPTER TWO

You are Here (But Why?)

We have a dual role, we humans. A dual purpose, to reign and reflect, given to us by God himself. *Let us make.* We are created, a part of God's creation. *In our image.* We are God's unique image bearers, his representatives here on earth.

CHAPTER TWO
You are Here (But Why?)

And now, little children, abide in him, so that when he appears we may have confidence and not shrink from him in shame at his coming.

I John 2:28

What is our goal in this life? We sometimes believe that it is to have enough, to do enough, to *be* enough. Scripture teaches that the ultimate goal, the glory of humanity, is to reign over creation and to reflect the praise of creation back to God.[11] When God created man, he spoke our purpose over us: "Then God said, 'Let us make mankind in our image, in our likeness ...'" We have a dual role, we humans. A dual purpose, to reign and reflect, given to us by God himself. *Let us make.* We are created, a part of God's creation. *In our image.* We are God's unique image bearers, his representatives here on earth.

Our first purpose is to reign over creation as God's image bearers. Being made in God's image brings with it certain responsibilities. The second part of Genesis 1:26 says that God decided we were to rule, to have dominion over, all living creatures. King David echoes this in Psalm 8 when he says that God crowned us with honor and made us rulers of all that God created.

"As God's image bearers ... we are to be wise stewards of the earth, caring for it and protecting it in a way that reflects and embodies God's rule over his creation."[12] As God's representatives, his image bearers, we also are to spread the knowledge of God and his love to the rest of the world. We are to work to speed up God's future goal for creation, to bring healing, restoration, hope, and peace to the world around us.

Our second role from that moment of creation is found in our very created-ness. *Let us make man in our image, in our likeness ...* We are created by God. Along with the trees, mountains, birds and sun, we ARE God's creation. We humans, however, have a unique role that was given to us on behalf of all of creation. A role that only we can fulfill. We are (as far as we know) the only creatures who can intelligently love God in return. We are the only part of creation who can give voice to the wordless praise of all creation.

"In the human being, creation finds a conscious answering voice, a mortal from the dust of the earth who can know and respond to God's love as a creature, love God in return, and as a part of this response, voice creation's praise."[13] This is a beautiful picture and a beautiful role that has been entrusted to us.

This, then, is what God created us to be and to do, and so our aim is to become the sort of humans God created us to be. Our *telos* (the Greek word for our purpose, our fulfillment, our vision of the good life toward which our whole being is aimed) is to become like the perfect human. It is to become like Jesus.

Yet how can we do this? I often find myself desperate to know God and to love him, to live in a way that loves all those around me, yet I simply cannot. So many days something ugly still wells up inside of me. Days when I want to be mean. Days when I feel resentful towards those I love best.

Some days my daughters cry to be held, fuss about wearing clothes, throw tantrums because school is hard, and my desire is not to comfort them but to scream like a crazed woman with fire in my eyes. Some days my husband makes an innocent comment, and my desire is not to hear his loving intentions but to deliberately misunderstand and hiss a disparaging remark. I intentionally fight to keep my dark mood. I want to savor, to wallow in my blackness. I hate these days.

When I, after more than 30 years of following Jesus, still have so many days like this, I find myself wondering how there can be any possibility at all of becoming like Jesus? When all of us find ourselves stumbling through each day, trying and failing, trying and failing again, how could anyone come even close?

This fairytale dream comes true through the grace of abiding. Through the death of Christ and the Holy Spirit in us, we are given the grace of abiding in Christ. Of becoming one with him.[14] Of looking into the face of God and being slowly, gently, brought to know him and in that knowing, to be made like him. We cannot try hard enough, we cannot try long enough, we can only abide. That's it.

Christos Yannaras, a theologian in the Orthodox Church, puts it this way: "To experience the personal otherness of a Creator Logos, Who is a passionate lover of mankind, is a revelation that is granted, not imposed. It cannot be gained as intellectual knowledge through the comprehension of a teaching, but only as an experience through the adventure of a revelation."[15] This, I believe, is key to this idea of abiding with Jesus. We cannot *do* anything at all to change ourselves into the image of Jesus. We can only *be*. The only thing given us is to continually place ourselves in the kind of space that allows God to transform our hearts. "Experience has taught the race that if [knowing] God is the end, then these habits of life are not the means but the condition in which the means operate."[16]

Living this God-life can only come from a place of being filled up with God. Being filled up with God can only come from abiding in him, waiting on the Lord, being still before him. Our ministry, our fruit, our very lives are not ours. They belong to God. Our only responsibility is to tend to our relationship with him. All else will flow from this: our direction, our mission, our fruit, our strength. Whatever it is that we think we want out of life, this abiding in Jesus is the only thing that will satisfy us. It is the only thing that will be enough.

This, then, is our ultimate goal, our *telos*: to know God and in knowing him to be made into the image of his Son. I am often in danger of losing sight of this goal. When we forget our *telos*, when we lose sight of who we truly were created to be, we are like the charioteer described by Athanasius, one of our church Fathers from the early 4th century. Athanasius' charioteer "paid no attention to the goal toward which he should be driving, but ... simply were to drive the horse as he could ...

and often drive against those he met, and often down steep places ... thinking that thus running he has not missed the goal — for he regards the running only and does not see that he has passed wide of the goal."[17]

It is an amusing image, the charioteer racing as quickly as he can, taking the most difficult paths and fighting against his fellow racers, only to miss the goal altogether. It is less amusing in the context of our own goal of knowing God.

Scripture tells us that God wants us to know him. He desires that we know him and love him far more than he desires half-hearted obedience.[18] He desires that our most gratifying success, the adventure that most fills our hearts with joy is to understand and know our Father.[19] This is what delights him.

Be still and know that I am God.[20]

Be still. We have convinced ourselves that to be busy should be our highest aim. We find a certain pride in telling others how busy we have been. Even our churches push us to serve more, attend more, *do* more. Yet this is not the teaching of Jesus. To abide is to dwell, to let go of everything and be with those we love. To abide is to become like Jesus's mother, Mary, who told the angel that God could do what he wished with her and then pondered it all quietly in her heart. To abide is to become like another Mary, who chose the better way by sitting quietly at the feet of Jesus. "Quietness is blessedness, ... quietness is strength, ... quietness is the source of the highest activity — the secret of all true abiding in Christ!"[21] Isaiah writes that "in returning and rest you shall be saved; in quietness and in trust shall be your strength."[22]

Be still and *know*. "To *know*. We've lost much of the richness of that word. Nowadays, "to know" means to know with the intellect. But it is a much deeper word than that. In the realm of faith, I *know* far more than I can believe with my finite mind."[23] In Hebrew, the language of the Old Testament, *yada*, and in Greek, the language of the New, *ginosko*: to know deeply and intimately.

There are truths we cannot know in words, truths we cannot reach with our minds. Be still, we are told. Be still and know. "There is a kind of knowing that comes in silence and not in words — but first we must be still."[24] Be still. In Hebrew it means to let go, to relax, to let drop. This is not our first instinct when we think of the God-life, when we think of how to bear fruit that pleases God. We instead want to figure out this transformation process, spit out the right formula, the best method for becoming like Jesus. Yet this is not what God asks of us. He instead simply asks us to be still. To abide like the branch abides in the vine and then to let him do the work. "As Jesus promised, the fruit will grow if we remain attached to the vine. Our job is to remain attached, to 'abide.'"[25]

This abiding, this knowing is what I desire most of all, what we all desire deep within ourselves. We are busy people living harried and overworked lives. We live surrounded by the chaos and distractions of our activities, our phones, the very fabric of our culture, and we are desperate for some stillness, some quiet, for some *thing* deeper and more than what we currently experience. We go and do and fill our lives with movement and sound and input and yet in times when we accidentally encounter a moment of quiet, we feel ... empty.

What I need, what we need, what all of us who are racing in the wrong direction need most of all in this moment is to be filled up with nothing less than God himself. We need the promised peace and joy of Jesus. We must create the space to gaze at the living Christ and to be made like him.

We must be still and know.

We must learn to abide.

Cultivating Rhythms

- Take some time in a quiet place to ask the Holy Spirit to show you what your goal in life has become. What do you want out of life? In what areas has your goal become doing enough or being enough in your own strength? Where have you found pride in your busyness? Sit with these questions quietly for a while. Ask God to mold your heart to desire the same goal that he desires for you. Ask him to refocus you so that you are aimed at the best goal.

- Do you deeply believe that God wants you to know him? Sit quietly with this idea and ask him to speak to you about that.

- Ask the Holy Spirit to show you where you are like Athanasius' charioteer who "paid no attention to the goal toward which he should be driving" but are driving a proverbial horse against those you meet, down steep places, and "thinking that thus running," you have not missed the goal. What can you do to slow down and see?

- On the flip side, also be sure to ask where you have shown that you are an image bearer of God, that you do love him, that you do worship and give voice to his praise. Remember, the Holy Spirit does not condemn (Rom. 8:1); it is good to acknowledge his faithful work in you, where you have seen glimmers of hope in the goal of life.

CHAPTER THREE

Abiding in the Wait: "My Thirst is Rising"

From the very start of our faith and all along the way, being alone with God has come before any service, any ministry, any fruit at all flowing out of lives. We must *first* spend time gazing at God and being filled up with himself.

CHAPTER THREE

Abiding in the Wait: "My Thirst is Rising"

The Lord is good to those who wait for him, to the soul who seeks him.

Lamentations 3:25

Be still.

Be still and wait.

Be still and wait for God.

Be still and wait for God to come.

A large piece of our abiding in Jesus is to be still and wait for him to come down and rescue us, change us, give us the grace of himself. When we are still, when we practice the habits of silence and solitude, we pause in the middle of our fighting and our striving, we rest from our grieving and our mourning, we stop to breathe in the midst of our busyness and our too much. Just for a moment.

The stillness doesn't take any of it away. Yet. But we become still like Moses with the Red Sea in front and the Egyptian army behind and we wait for God to fight for us. We wait for God to change us. We wait for God, and in that waiting, in the stillness, we come to *know* God. "Stillness is a precondition to deep knowing of God."[26] In knowing God, which is too often confused with knowing *about* God, we are changed.

David Benner, a Canadian author and psychologist, argues that being transformed through prayer happens most and best in stillness: "A life of prayer that is exclusively built around attending, pondering and responding will not have the same transformational possibilities as that which also includes times for simply being with God ... stillness before God in silence."[27]

We are all hurried and busy and weary. Our world (and even our churches) insist that we accomplish more, that we *be* more. Our culture proclaims that our value comes from what we do. Our churches declare that grateful people give of themselves to others through service, that in serving you will feel close to God. Everything around us instills within our deepest places that we are to *do* rather than *be*. It is enough to exhaust anyone. What happened to *Come to me, all who labor and are heavy laden, and I will give you rest*?[28]

Yet what if we have this all backward? What if being still in the presence of God is the practice from which all the others flow? What if this is the well from which all else in this God-life streams rather than our frantic efforts of service, no matter how well-intentioned, being the vehicle that brings us into the presence of God?

While I do not believe that anyone would have stated it so baldly, the idea that service is what strengthens our faith and makes us more like Jesus, that if you do nothing else you should at least be serving, was certainly implied in most of the churches I have attended.

This is a working farm.

If everyone would find their place to serve, fewer people would be over-burdened.

Our children need you to volunteer in the student program!

Yet so many of the Fathers and Mothers of our faith have said otherwise. From the very start of our faith and all along the way, being alone with God has come before any service, any ministry, any fruit flowing out of our lives at all. We must *first* spend time gazing at God and being filled up with himself.

Listen as our church Fathers and Mothers speak to us from the very beginning of the Church until the present day:

Moses spent time with God on the mountain as he led the people.[29] Daniel prayed three times a day, even when it got him thrown into the lions' den.[30] Shepherd-king David prayed through every human emotion, comparing himself to a deer panting for flowing streams of water in his thirst for God.[31] The apostles spent time together before God before choosing a replacement for Judas.[32] Jesus himself regularly removed himself from the crowds to be with his Father alone.[33] It was out of these times of silence and solitude that Christ's ministry streamed.

Gregory of Nyssa, a church Father from the 4th century, taught from the life of Moses that "he who desires to behold God sees the object of his longing in always following him. The contemplation of his face is the unending journey accomplished by following directly behind the Word."[34]

Teresa of Avila, a Spanish Carmelite nun from the 16th century, is known for her writings on prayer. Others spoke of her as bringing God with her wherever she went in service of others. Teresa wrote that anyone who wants to know God "has no need to go to heaven to speak to her eternal Father and enjoy his presence...all she needs is to be alone and contemplate him in herself..."[35]

Hear nineteenth century Methodist author E. M. Bounds (who wrote an astonishing nine books on prayer!): "A holy life would not be so rare or so difficult a thing if our devotions were not so short and hurried ... Our ability to stay with God in our closet measures our ability to stay with God out of the closet."[36]

Henri Nouwen, a priest and theologian from the second half of the 20th century, spoke of silence and solitude as practices that were intertwined. He wrote that "solitude is the furnace of transformation ... Silence is the discipline by which the inner fire of God is tended and kept alive."[37]

Ruth Haley Barton, writing in the early 21st century, writes that waiting on God (not to show up, for he is always here, but to fill us up with himself) in silence and solitude is the only way that we can serve in compassion without being overwhelmed, the only way we can serve in a way that truly glorifies him. "If we relax and trust God's initiative in the spiritual process, ... a different capacity for being present to others in love comes upon us, almost imperceptibly at first. Far beyond the familiar territory of 'ought' and 'should,' we may notice a spontaneous and surprising desire to find a way to bring some of what we are experiencing in God's presence to others."[38]

This idea is not a new approach to "doing ministry." It is not a way to "do more for God." Being silent and alone before God, waiting on him (sometimes for years) to fill us up with his presence and then give us our one next step of obedience is the way His most trusted servants have practiced loving God and loving others since the very beginning.

It is a common thread not only throughout time but woven among all faith traditions that silence and solitude are an important piece of what makes us fully human, of what helps us to be as we were created to be. Thomas Merton, a monk and theologian from the first half of the 20th century, wrote of silence and solitude being necessary for the fullness of human living.[39] Bishop Kallistos Ware, a priest and theologian for our Orthodox brothers and sisters, wrote that "to believe that man is made in God's image is to believe that man is created for communion and union with God, and that if he rejects this communion he ceases to be properly man."[40]

Andrew Murray writes much of quietness before God in both shorter daily times and in longer regular times away. "Abide in Christ! Let no one think that he can do this if he has not daily his quiet time, his seasons of meditation and waiting on God." Shorter daily time and longer times away — both are necessary. I could write so much more about the idea of retreat, or wilderness time, that is beyond the scope of this book. I will provide more resources at the end for those who thirst for more.

The idea of waiting on God, of being still before him, is also a major practice all through the Old Testament. The Psalms are filled with the idea of waiting on God. Jeremiah writes in Lamentations that "the Lord is good to those who wait for him, to the soul who seeks him." The first time I read these words from the prophet Isaiah, my eyes filled with tears of sorrow: "For thus said the Lord God, the Holy One of Israel, 'In returning and rest you shall be saved; in quietness and in trust shall be your strength.' But you were unwilling..." I have long been unwilling, and still have times of being unwilling, yet more and more I find myself returning to God in rest, in quietness, in trust. When I do, I find strength and salvation.

I still feel very much a beginner at practicing these intertwined disciplines of silence and solitude (I am learning, however, that even those who have practiced these things for decades still call themselves beginners!), yet here are a few practices that have been helpful to me as I began this journey:

Remove all distractions, especially your phone, and be truly alone. Be gracious to yourself in whatever season of life you find yourself. Perhaps my most difficult season thus far was being at home with very little ones. Start small. If a few minutes at your desk at lunch or while your littles are napping and your bigs are on the couch with a book is all you can manage, start there. You can always increase your time by a minute or two later on.

When stray thoughts come, don't fret but simply release them into God's care and do not dwell on them. Use a phrase like the Jesus prayer (The long version: "Lord Jesus Christ, Son of God, have mercy on me a sinner." The short version: "Lord Jesus, have mercy on me.") to bring your thoughts back to their focus when they begin to drift. Henri Nouwen writes, "A word of sentence repeated frequently can help us to concentrate, to move to the center, to create an inner stillness and thus listen to the voice of God."[41] I use a series of three phrases from British author Elizabeth Goudge: "Lord have mercy. Thee I adore. Into Thy hands." Sometimes I repeat them all. Sometimes I feel led to just one.

It will feel awkward at first. This is normal. I found myself distracted by every noise, every flash in my peripheral vision, found my mind wandering far before I remembered to drag it back, found myself wondering whether anything at all had happened. I learned to set a timer so that I did not spend my time glancing at my watch every two minutes, believing I had been quiet for hours.

Now? Sometimes it still feels awkward. And sometimes I come away with a hunger for more.

Lastly, know yourself. Know the way God created you. If you can sit just quietly with only a candle to focus your thoughts, that is what you should do. If you focus best when you are creating with your hands, sit with paper and colors or yarn and needles. If your body must move in order for your mind to be still, take yourself out to the woods or the streets of your neighborhood. God created you perfectly and desires you to be still in exactly the way He made you to be. Only do so. Do so regularly. Do what you can and then little by little, every so often, add a little more. It is not easy; I won't pretend that it is. I will write more about that a little further on — but know that solitude is hard work. In the beginning you may experience restlessness, emptiness, anxiety. Take heart and press on. With time, you will find freedom, peace, fulfillment, transformation.

For now, let me give you a glimpse of my own heart about a year into beginning this practice of silence and solitude:

> I am learning to listen, to sit in silence and wait.
>
> I mostly come away disappointed, and yet ...
>
> I mostly come away without a word, and yet ...
>
> I mostly come away feeling a failure, and yet ...
>
> My thirst is growing.
>
> I am learning to listen, to sit in silence and wait.
>
> I strain to know his thoughts, but mostly my own still swarm like a plague of gnats.
>
> I seek to hear his words, but mostly my own still darken my way.
>
> I long to comprehend His desires and plans, but mostly my own still lead me astray.
>
> And yet ...
>
> My thirst is mounting.
>
> Outwardly nothing changes.
>
> There is no voice from heaven.
>
> There is no flood of emotion.
>
> There is no flash of understanding.
>
> And yet ...

Inwardly something is stirring.

Nothing grand,

Nothing immense,

Only the beginnings of a something is stirring.

Mostly there is nothing.

And yet ...

My thirst is rising.

I am learning to listen, to sit in silence and wait.

Cultivating Rhythms

- Spend some time thinking about the practice of being still and silent with God. In what ways do you feel yourself embracing this idea? In what ways do you feel yourself resisting this idea? Ask the Holy Spirit to show you what he wants you to do with this practice.

- Start where you are and ask God to help you figure out where you can add to your practice of silence and solitude. If you have never practiced this before, find five to 10 minutes each day to begin. If you have practiced this for years, add a few minutes to your time.

- Take three deep breaths to relax. You can close your eyes, or you can focus on something such as a candle or cross. Ask the Spirit to help you be still. Clear your mind. As thoughts arise, use your breath prayer or name of God to gently push them away. If you journal, it can be helpful to write them down as a way to move them aside. Set a timer so that you can free yourself from peeking at the clock every few moments. End by thanking God for being with you. He was there and he accomplished everything he wanted to accomplish, regardless of how you feel at the end.

- As was suggested, try different methods of being still (going for a walk outside or coloring and doodling, if you need your body or hands to be busy in order for your mind to be still) based on your own personality and interests. If one way doesn't work for you, try another. But give it time. This is not an easy practice, but it is a necessary one.

CHAPTER FOUR

Lectio Divina: Drink Deeply

Allowing the Word to form us by the slow revealing of himself through the slow inhalation of the words of Scripture. This is *lectio divina*. It is the deep and slow reading of a phrase or word of Scripture with the intention of plunging deeply rather than consuming widely. It is the holy use of our sacred imagination to become immersed in the Word and to be formed by it.

CHAPTER FOUR

Lectio Divina: Drink Deeply

If you abide in my word, you are truly my disciples.

John 8:31

In the beginning, God spoke. God spoke his Word and his Word created. God's Word created the intense, white heat of the sun and the cool, silver silence of the moon. He created stately, rooted, aged trees and coarse, prickly, waving sea grass. He created ordinary, brown, song-filled sparrows and majestic, golden, prowling lions. Nothing exists that was not created through him. Life exploded and revealed God to man. The life of the heavens and the life of the earth revealed his invisible qualities to all who cared to look. It is the nature of words and the nature of the Word to reveal.

Jesus is the Word and he spoke the words that revealed God to man.[42] The Word revealed the heart of God far more than life ever could. As people received the Word made flesh, new life exploded into being. The Word formed the people into new life, into a new creation. This new creation then spoke the same Word and new life again blazed out.

As we hear and receive the Word, we are formed by the Word. This is *lectio divina*. Allowing the Word to form us by the slow revealing of himself through the slow inhalation of the words of Scripture. It is the deep and slow reading of a phrase or word of Scripture with the intention of plunging deeply rather than consuming widely. It is the holy use of our sacred imagination to become immersed in the Word and to be formed by it.

Richard Foster, one of the foremost theologians and writers on spiritual formation in our time, makes the bold claim that "the ancient Christian practice of *lectio divina* is the primary mode of reading the Bible for transformation."[43] I will confess that I was skeptical of this, even from someone whose Biblical authority I trust as much as Foster. Perhaps many of you glance sideways at this as well. After all, this is not something that is often taught in our Western, Protestant, Evangelical, non-denominational churches. Yet I kept coming across similar declarations from other scholars whom I trust.

Hear two more testimonies:

Dallas Willard, an American philosopher and theologian known for his writings on Christian spiritual formation, wrote that reading Scripture in this way allows us to have a few verses of the Word "transferred *into the substance of our lives*" as opposed to having every piece of the Bible flash before our eyes. This is how we come to have part of the mind of Christ in us as our own. "We are fitted out then to function as true co-laborers with God as brothers, sisters and friends of Jesus in the present and coming kingdom of God. And we are in a position to know and understand fully how God speaks now to his children."[44]

Eugene Peterson, an American Presbyterian minister, author, and poet, writes that *lectio divina* "is not a methodical technique for reading the

Bible. It is a cultivated, developed habit of *living* the text in Jesus' name. This is the way, the *only* way, that the Holy Scriptures become formative in the Christian church and become salt and leaven in the world."[45]

Lectio divina is not a new discipline, a trend that will eventually fade back into the shadows again. This way of reading Scripture has been practiced since the beginnings of our Christian faith. God instructs Joshua to meditate on his law day and night.[46] The Psalms, in particular, are full of this idea. *I will meditate on your precepts.*[47] *My eyes are awake before the watches of the night, that I may meditate on your promise.*[48] *I meditate on all you have done.*[49] The two Hebrew words translated as meditate, *hagah* and *siyach*, mean to muse, to ponder, to imagine. One image is of a lion growling and muttering over his prey — chewing deep into something until you reach the marrow of the bone. This is not some other-worldly trance but a long and deep rumination, a chewing the cud, of the Word.

The Jewish practice was to pray, among other prayers, a cycle of the Psalms and the *Shema* from Deuteronomy 6:4-7 (both wonderful places to begin practicing *lectio divina*), and this habit carried over into the early Church. It was practiced by many of the earliest church Fathers, including Ambrose, one of the most influential Church leaders in the middle of the 4th century, and Augustine, Ambrose's student, who left an indelible mark on the Church.

It is practiced not only by our Western Church brothers and sisters, but by our Eastern family as well. Bishop Kallistos Ware, an Orthodox theologian, wrote that "the study of words (in Scripture) should give place to an immediate dialogue with the living Word himself. 'Whenever you read the Gospel,' says St. Tikhon of Zadonsk, 'Christ himself is speaking to you. And while you read, you are praying and talking with him.'"[50] The Orthodox Church even practices *lectio divina* corporately, using the liturgical services to "feed the spiritual imagination of the worshipper" using the length and frequent repetitions of the Biblical texts.[51]

Lectio divina is a way of engaging our sacred imagination, of abiding in Jesus and allowing his words to abide in us. It is a way for God to transform our deepest selves by giving us a vision of who he is and who he created us to be.

Take a look at Isaiah. The Old Testament prophet of God who saw the glory of Christ. The man who named his sons to teach a lesson, who outlasted many kings, who pled with Israel over and over to turn back to her God. Isaiah.

Yet before his passioned *Here I am! Send me.*[52] acceptance of God's call, even before God's call rings out for someone, anyone to go and speak for him, Isaiah is given a vision. He is given a vision of God on his throne, high and exalted, with the train of his robe filling the temple. Before the call can be heard and accepted, the vision that changes everything must be seen.

A vision of God is what changed Isaiah, what inspired him to take on the enormously difficult task of delivering God's message.

Vision requires imagination. Sacred imagination. Too often we want to go straight to the take-away, straight to the studying and the parsing and the exegesis, straight to our to-do list. Instead, we must pause. We must be still. We must drink deeply rather than skimming widely. We must let God inspire us and change our hearts by filling our imaginations with a vision of him. Most of us will never experience Isaiah's variety of vision, yet all of us are gifted with some degree of imagination that can bring us into the presence of God and allow us to "see" him in our minds and hearts, thus causing us to fall more deeply in love with this holy, glorious, beautiful God.

In *lectio divina*, we come to our reading as to a holy meeting with God, praying for God's Holy Spirit to bring his words fully into our hearts and into our lives. We read the text slowly, pausing often to perhaps close our eyes, tip our heads back, but always to ponder deeply what we have read, allowing the words to slip into our blood and bones, into our very life. We read in humility and submission, asking God to speak to us through his Word and desiring that his revealed will should be true for us as it was for the original authors.

One way to practice *lectio divina* is to begin humbly, with a familiar text. Read it. Ponder it. Pray it. Live it. Spiral in and out and around those ways as you read. Most of all, read it in an act of love for the One who speaks the words.

This is a practice in which it has not taken quite so long for me to see fruit. Fruit is still slow in growing, as fruit is wont to do, and some days I suspect that the fruit has receded back into the vine a bit, yet many days

I am able to sense at least a piece of what God wants to say to me. As I read a small portion of Scripture slowly, going over it multiple times with space in between, often one word or phrase will stand out to me. I dwell on that word or phrase, thinking it over, making connections to other pieces of Scripture, holding it in stillness before God, listening to what he might want to say to me through that word or phrase, and thinking what I want to say to God about it. Through it all I find myself filled up with him.

I will caution that in this, as in all things, balance is needed. We must not read Scripture only for formation any more than we should read only for information. There is a need to move back and forth between studying Scripture — the meanings of the original language and how that fits together with the historical context, searching for threads of connection that flow through the whole, and gaining an understanding of the nature and character of God — *and* the deep and slow meditation of Scripture — waiting for God to speak through his own words, granting us a vision of Himself, and thus forming us in the image of his Son.

Eugene Peterson writes of exegesis (the study of a passage using the original language, historical context, literary genre, etc.) as an act of love: "It loves the one who speaks the words enough to want to get the words right. It respects the words enough to use every means we have to get the words right."[53] Getting the words right and being formed by the words are both needed.

This is the way we receive the Word made flesh and are formed into a new creation. This is the way we become so filled up with a vision of the Word that we are able to then speak the same Word into others so that new life again will blaze out.

Cultivating Rhythms

- Begin this practice using a piece of Scripture with which you are already familiar. The Lord's Prayer, Matthew 22:37-40, Psalm 23 — all of these are good places to begin.

- Take three deep breaths to relax, ask the Holy Spirit to guide you, and read the verse or short passage once slowly. Pause and listen. What word or phrase stands out to you? What images come to mind? Be still and listen to what God might want to say to you through these words.

- Read the passage a second time. Allow your head and heart to work together this time. What thoughts and images arise? What connections to other pieces of Scripture do you make? What emotions come up in your heart?

- Read the passage a third time. Respond to what you have been hearing and thinking and feeling. What do you want to say to God about this? You may respond with words and you may respond in a feeling or emotion.

- Read the passage a fourth time. Simply be still and know the God who has spoken to you through the Word. End by thanking God.

- If this practice is still new and uncomfortable to you, take heart. It was uncomfortable for me at first too. It helped me to remember that it is a discipline our early church Fathers and Mothers pulled out of Scripture itself. Do a search in the Bible for the word "meditate" or "meditation" and see what you find. Let the Holy Spirit speak to you about this.

CHAPTER FIVE

The Cure for the Sickness of Busy

Having rhythms of being alone with God and his word are the way we are healed by the Holy Spirit from this illness of being busy. Having rhythms of taking time out of our busyness to gaze at the Lord, taking the time to sit at his feet and learn how to abide in him, making our home in him, this is the cure for our illness.

CHAPTER FIVE
The Cure for the Sickness of Busy

Be still before the Lord and wait patiently for him.

Psalm 37:7

None of these practices, these rhythms of abiding, happen without making time for them, yet time is mostly what we do not have. Our culture has instilled in us a pride in our busyness. We brag about how little free time we have, how many vacation days we have built up from disuse, how many activities in which we have involved our children. We feel, in fact, a sense of shame if we don't have work or play scheduled on the weekends. We run and we hurry and in the middle of our running and hurrying we wonder how in the world — how in this fretful, busy world — we could possibly still feel empty. So we ramp up the running and the hurrying in an attempt to drown out the loneliness. Why is it so hard to jump off this carousel?

Paul Jensen, founder and director of The Leadership Institute and assistant professor at Fuller Theological Seminary, has spent much of his time researching the way our culture has collapsed time and space. From the advent of common time in the 1880's to keep trains running on schedule to more modern technology that allows us to virtually enter any time or space, we organize the whole of our lives around technologies that allow us to be more efficient and productive. We want to cram more and more into our schedules. Regardless of how full our lives are, however, we are increasingly empty inside. "Busyness acts to repress our inner fears and personal anxieties, as we scramble to achieve an enviable image to display to others. We become 'outward' people obsessed with how we appear, rather than 'inward' people, reflecting on the meaning of our lives."[54]

We have bought into a belief system, both in our world and in our churches, that says our worth as a person is dependent on our accomplishments. Brené Brown, a research professor in social work, writes of the way we use busyness to escape our feelings of isolation and powerlessness. We want to find better ways of managing our exhaustion and anxiety. "We want help 'living like this,' not suggestions on how to 'stop living like this.'"[55] Because if we stop living like this, we are forced to face our shame, face our fear that we are not enough. For women, setting boundaries is difficult because the shame gremlins are quick to weigh in: 'Careful saying no. You'll really disappoint these folks. Don't let them down. Be a good girl. Make everyone happy.' For men, the gremlins whisper, 'Man up. A real guy could take this on and then some. Is the little mamma's boy just too tired?'"[56] We attempt to use our busyness to soothe our anxiety, which simply does not work. We might be able to cover those feelings for a while, but soon enough find our tension spiraling out of control.

Even (especially?) in our churches, we are infected with this disease.

We try to put mission first, to spur people on to serve before teaching them to wait on God's leading. We rush in front of the Holy Spirit and then wonder why our ideas do not work and why our compassion turns into exhaustion. We cannot give out of our emptiness with any lasting strength. It is easy to become weary of compassion when we are not waiting on God to take the lead. "It is probably a matter of time before the intensity of suffering in others leads us to harden our hearts against it. After all, there is only so much suffering any of us can take before we are simply overwhelmed by it."[57]

Our only chance, then, to participate in any Kingdom ministry, to bear the fruit of love and compassion in our lives, is to allow our ministry to come *only* out of abiding. We must wait for God to fill us up with himself[58] so that it is his love and his compassion that flow out of us, rather than our own ideas about what ought to be done.

"Only God in Christ can take on the suffering of the world in compassion and not be destroyed by it. Only God can heal the world's brokenness. All ministry is God's ministry, or, more accurately, God's ministry in Jesus Christ, to the glory of the Father, in the power of the Spirit, for the sake of the world ... this means accepting our responsibility to attend to our relationship with Christ, a relationship established and maintained by him, recognizing that outside of that relationship we have no way of participating in God's ongoing ministry to the world."[59]

Any action at all in our churches, any ministry that happens outside of our churches, must be God's. Abiding comes first.

Jensen's research reveals a surprising contradiction to the idea that we need to prune our lives of all busyness, however. The truth, it turns out, is more nuanced than that. The truth is that busyness is not always a negative occurrence *as long as* you have regular rhythms of stillness in place in your life as well. The problem comes when you have a life that is full of busyness with a complete dearth of any times of stillness.

Jesus' own life shows this rhythm of ministry busyness and alone-with-God stillness. A rhythm in which both busyness and stillness involve an intimate connection with God. When we read the gospels, we discover his almost constant action throughout — coming, going, crowding, teaching, healing — *and* Jesus is regularly withdrawing from all of this activity, regularly going to a place of solitude to pray.

Rhythm.

When our lives are full of work and activity with no times of respite, we become exhausted and anxious. When we have an overabundance of time, we become bored and struggle to find purpose in life.[60]

Rhythm.

God taught us about rhythms at the very beginning of the nation of Israel. In the same passage later quoted by Jesus as the Greatest Commandment, Moses is giving instruction about when they arrive in the Promised Land. *Hear, O Israel: The LORD our God, the LORD is one.* Moses tells the people they should keep God in their hearts and minds, they should talk about God, talk to God, listen to God, both when they are still and when they are busy. ... *when you sit in your house and when you walk by the way ...* [61]

Rhythm.

Some seasons do not hold a natural rhythm. The early years of parenting, the later years of parent-care. How do you find rhythms of being still when there is no stillness to be found? How do you find space in your day when there seems to be no space to be found?

When I was nursing babies, I would use those times to be still with God. I would often fall asleep, often the prayer was not much more than *God, help,* but he took what I had to offer, even though it was not very much in those days, and like the loaves and the fish, transformed it into just what I needed to make it through my day.

Now, with a house full of homeschooled elementary and junior high kids, I carve out time at the beginning and the end of the day. I set the alarm on my phone to remind me to pray at nine in the morning, at noon, and at three in the afternoon. Some days, I confess, I silence the alarm and continue as though nothing had happened. Some days I simply whisper a breath prayer. "Lord have mercy. Thee I adore. Into Thy hands." Some days I get down on my knees for a few minutes. If nothing else, the alarm pulls my heart back toward God.

Rhythm.

You begin by asking the One who created time to help you order your time. You begin by asking God to open your eyes to tiny pockets of time throughout your day. You do not have to begin with three-hour blocks of time. You *should not* begin with three-hour blocks of time.

Start small. A dear friend once told me that if we do still ourselves for small bits of time, God has a fighting chance of showing us what we can say "no" to in order to make more room for him.

Rhythm.

This is why these disciplines of silence and solitude and *lectio divina* are so necessary to our lives. Having rhythms of being alone with God and his Word are the way we are healed by the Holy Spirit from this illness of being busy. Daily rhythms, as well as longer monthly and annual rhythms, of being still are the way we put ourselves in a place where God can fill us up with himself. Having rhythms of taking time out of our busyness to gaze at the Lord, taking the time to sit at his feet and learn how to abide in him, making our home in him, this is the cure for our illness.

Cultivating Rhythms

- Spend some time praying about your daily rhythms. Think through your days and pay attention to which pieces bring you life and which bring a dangerous kind of exhaustion. Ask the Holy Spirit to bring to your mind creative ways to create rhythms of abiding throughout your day. As difficult as it is to cut activities and tasks out of your day, don't neglect to ask the Spirit for discernment into what he is asking you to give up.

- Begin where you are. If you have no rhythms in place yet, perhaps finding a short verse or a name of God to meditate on throughout your day is a good place to start. If you already have rhythms at the beginning or close of your day, consider how to add a rhythm at the other end. Consider ways to bring your mind back to God regularly throughout your day. Use technology to your benefit.

- Through all of this, ask the Holy Spirit to guide you; do not rely on your own strength. Immerse this process of considering your rhythms in prayer.

CHAPTER SIX

Finding the Holy and Hidden Heart of our Daily Routine

Jesus tells us to abide in his love and to abide in his words. Taking the time daily to be still with him and his Word is the way we remain attached to the Vine, becoming one with Christ as he is one with the Father.

CHAPTER SIX
Finding the Holy and Hidden Heart of our Daily Routine

If you keep my commandments, you will abide in my love.

John 15:10

Life. Paul says that Christ is before all things and that in him all things hold together,[62] yet it is difficult to believe that God could be a part of something as ordinary as cleaning toilets, as tedious as reading yet one more rendition of *Goodnight Moon*. Yet if we are to abide in Christ, these are exactly the kinds of activities where we are to look for him. If God is present in the singing of a hymn, he is also present in the folding of a spouse's shirt.

A.W. Tozer, in *The Pursuit of God*, directs our eyes to Jesus, pointing out that if Christ's claim is true that he only does what pleases the Father, then this would also include such prosaic activities as eating, sleeping, and being with friends. We hesitate to include these earthy concerns in a list of what can be called sacred, and Paul seems to anticipate our hesitation. *Whether you eat or drink, or whatever you do.*[63] We even eat and drink to the glory of God.

When we look to Jesus and the life that he lived, we see the same. All that he did was pleasing to the Father. In everything, he obeyed the Father's commands.[64] God means for all of life to be sacred, for the mundane as well as the important to be done in a way that glorifies him.

When we become one with Jesus by abiding with him, we become able to do the work of the Father as his Spirit flows through the Vine into us. By doing the work that God gives us as excellently as we can, we are bringing Kingdom rule (God's will be done) and glory into the space in which we live.

Andrew Murray, in *Abide in Christ*, writes about the progressive renewal of the Holy Spirit that leads to our having the very mind of Christ which allows us to understand the meaning and application of God's commands within our daily lives.[65] This renewal allows us to become like jazz musicians.

A jazz pianist, a really good one, knows his art intimately. It is a part of his spirit. When he plays with a band, he understands the fundamentals of how music behaves. He knows the nature of the musical form; he knows the structure of the harmonics well enough to think quickly and compose something in that very moment that fits in with the reality of the music. The improvisation is so seamless it appears as though he had spent weeks composing it ahead of time.

This is how I want to live — improvising my life as beautifully as jazz. I want to know God and how he has created the nature of this life and this world well enough to know how to respond no matter what is happening around me. I want to be able to react so seamlessly that it appears I had spent weeks thinking through my reaction ahead of time. I want to have the mind of Christ. "Love will assimilate into your inmost being the commands as food from heaven. They will no longer come to you as a law standing outside and against you, but as the living power which has transformed your will into perfect harmony with all your Lord requires."[66]

"Of such a one it may be said that every act of his life is or can be as truly sacred as prayer or baptism or the Lord's Supper. To say this is not to bring all acts down to one dead level; it is rather to lift every act up into a living kingdom and turn the whole life into a sacrament."[67]

Turn the whole life into a sacrament. It is a beautiful idea and one that fits perfectly with Scripture. God clearly cares about the menial details of our lives. Anyone who doubts this only needs to read the book of Leviticus.

In Leviticus, God gives minute instructions to the Israelites concerning how to go about daily life, from how to care for articles of clothing to how to work in a vineyard. He tells them how to clean cooking pots that have come in contact with an insect and what to do when their tent gets moldy. He tells those who work the land not to harvest the fields too thoroughly but to leave a little for the poor.

God our Father does indeed care about every moment; he cares about even our everyday routine. He cares so much about us that he wants to be present to us in everything we do, not in order to control every little decision we make (remember living like a jazz musician?), but simply to *be* with us. He wants us to make our home in him, to abide in him.

God makes, it turns out, no separation between sacred and secular. All is made sacred and all is in Christ. So how do we become awake to his presence in our daily lives? How do we learn to abide in Jesus so that we have no place of our lives in which he does not dwell, no place in which we walk without dwelling in him? After all, as British author Evelyn Underhill says in *The Spiritual Life*, "The spiritual life is simply the life in which all we do comes from the centre, where we are anchored in God."[68] Our lives are so full, so full of necessary things that demand our attention. How can we possibly stay attuned to God all around us? How do we live anchored to God?

I have found the answer to this to be largely, though not entirely, through the spiritual disciplines. Specifically, in the context of learning to abide, through silence and solitude and through *lectio divina*. As we have seen, Jesus tells us to abide in his love and to abide in his words.[69] Taking the time daily to be still with him and his Word is the way we remain attached to the Vine, becoming one with Christ as he is one with the Father. "What we only need is this: to take time and study the divine image of this life of love set before us in Christ. We need to have our souls still unto God, gazing upon that life of Christ in the Father until the light from heaven falls on it, and we hear the living voice of our Beloved whispering gently to us personally the teaching He gave to the disciples."[70]

As we practice these holy habits, we learn to become aware of God's presence in every area of our lives. We wake up to God's presence and his purposes in our lives and our world. Rather than going through our days mindful only of the world we can see, as we weave in these holy habits, we become more fully conscious of how completely intertwined are the physical and spiritual worlds.

A.W. Tozer speaks of this intertwining in *The Pursuit of God*. He says that the spiritual world is real in the same sense that the visible world is real. "We must break the evil habit of ignoring the spiritual. We must shift our interest from the seen to the unseen."[71] Tozer tells us that the Kingdom of God is not some distant future promise, but a present reality, a parallel to the seen world. Disciplining ourselves to gaze at God in our silent times with him helps the eyes of our soul see this Kingdom everywhere we turn. When we yield ourselves to his discipline and submit ourselves to him, our whole life becomes one with him. We abide in him.

Brother Lawrence, a seventeenth century monk, understood this. Brother Lawrence was not the most important monk in the monastery; on the contrary, he was the dishwasher. This dishwasher for an entire monastery certainly knew how commonplace and uninteresting such tasks could be, yet his thoughts and writings about living in the presence of God at all times, even while washing dishes, influenced many around him and have continued to influence Christ-followers to this day.[72]

For Brother Lawrence, standing at the kitchen sink was just as sacred, just as holy and pleasing to God, as kneeling at the altar. Both were opportunities to commune with Christ in an uninterrupted fellowship, both brought him a flow of peace as ceaseless as a river. As a monk, Brother Lawrence would certainly have spent regular times in silence and solitude, and it would have been a habit for him to practice *lectio divina*; he learned how to bring this learned awareness of God's abiding presence into his daily work.

He observed in a collection of his letters, *Practicing the Presence of God*, that "the time of business does not differ with me from the time of prayer; and in the noise and clatter of my kitchen, while several persons are at the same time calling for different things, I possess God in as great tranquility as if I were upon my knees at the blessed sacrament."[73]

In the same passage from the gospel of John in which Jesus speaks of abiding in him, he reminds us that "apart from me you can do nothing" (John 15:5). Whether you are able to find large spaces of time in which to practice these habits regularly or whether you simply wrap your day around them through small ways (setting your phone to remind you to pause and focus on God for a moment every hour, perhaps, or finding a phrase or even just a word of Scripture or a name of God to meditate on all through your day, for example), God the Holy Spirit uses this regular abiding in him to increase our dependence on him. It forces us to rely on God to provide for this day only.

God transforms us in the now, through the present moment rather than the past or the future, and this sacred routine keeps us rooted in this present moment when we mostly desire either to dwell in the past or fret about the future. 16th century English humanist and statesman Thomas More spoke of the sacredness of this routine when he said, "the ordinary acts we practice every day at home are of more importance to the soul than their simplicity might suggest."

Theologian Frederick Buechner also spoke of ordinary life as a fathomless mystery. He admonishes us to listen to the ordinary, everyday life and see it for what it truly is: "In the boredom and pain of it no less than in the excitement and gladness: touch, taste, smell your way to the holy and hidden heart of it because in the last analysis all moments are key moments, and life itself is grace."[74]

When we find our way to the holy and hidden heart of our daily routine, we find that Jesus truly is before all things, that Christianity is not compartmentalized and relegated to a few hours on Sunday. Our Christian faith is a way of life. If we are to make our home in Christ, we must remain close to him at all times. The cold of the world is quick to seep into our very marrow when we move away from the fire of His Spirit. If we cannot learn to abide with Jesus in our daily routine, it will be difficult to cling to him when storms drive us out of our routine. This abiding is a way of doing life, a way of living life in relationship to the One who is the way, the truth, and the life.

I will add my own testimony to all of these wise, deeply experienced voices. As I have written several times already, it is a slow process, yet the more I have added sacred rhythms into my day, whether it be small moments consistently throughout the day or larger scheduled times at the beginning or ending of my days, whether it be a couple of hours walking in the woods once a month or a yearly weekend retreat, I am slowly waking up to God's presence with me. I find my thoughts turning to him more often throughout the day; I find my heart more tuned to the way in which he is working in my life and the lives of my family; I find myself more fully abiding at Home. It is beautiful and I find myself longing for more.

God asks not for a few hours on Sunday. He asks not even for a few moments each day. He is Lord, and he demands nothing less than all of us. It seems arduous, yet he promises that his burden is light. He will do all the work of keeping us close to himself if we will only take the time to simply be still and know, to gaze at him and his Word in silence.

We will discover, after all, that we find our greatest joy and our deepest peace on those days during which we are most successful in inviting him into *every moment* of our day. We find, too, that his command to abide in him is, in the end, a promise. A promise that one day we will be fully his, transformed to be fully like him, and we cooperate with this transformation as we do the things that Jesus did, watching to see what his habits and practices were and imitating them.

Christ is before all things, even cleaning toilets and standing at kitchen sinks, and in him all things hold together. All things were created by him and for him. If all things are created, then all things are sacred and can be used by God to awaken us to his presence and to transform us into his likeness.

Cultivating Rhythms

- As you sit in stillness with God, ask the Spirit to show you which pieces of your day you have not yet invited him into. Pay attention to your own spirit. Do you feel a longing for God to be an intimate part of every part of your day? Are there any bits of your day about which you feel a resistance to opening to God? Talk with God about that.

- The next time you find yourself in a repetitive household chore (like sorting laundry or loading the dishwasher), bring your mind to the holy and hidden heart of daily routine. Does this change your perspective of the task? How?

- Ask the Holy Spirit to give you wisdom and discernment in your daily routines. Are you in a season that gives you space for a large amount of time with God? Is your season one in which you must create smaller bits of time scattered throughout your day? Is there a way to make space for both? Have grace with yourself whichever season you are currently in.

CHAPTER SEVEN

Abiding in Suffering: Refuge in the Storm

By practicing the killing off of our sin nature through the chosen suffering of self-denial, our spiritual muscles are strengthened, and we are better able to cling to Jesus when suffering comes to us unbidden.

CHAPTER SEVEN

Abiding in Suffering: Refuge in the Storm

For thus said the Lord God, the Holy One of Israel,
"In returning and rest you shall be saved..."

Isaiah 30:15-18

It is this abiding in Christ in our daily routines that keeps us safe in him when storms come. And make no mistake: storms will come. This universal experience of pain is part of what makes us human, part of what makes us feel a kinship with each other. Jesus certainly did not try to deceive us about our lives as we follow him. Quite the opposite, he promised that storms would come.[75] He also promised us peace and joy in the middle of those storms.[76]

When we have made Jesus our home through the mundane, yet sacred, routines of daily life, when we have spent much time gazing at him and being filled up by him through silence, solitude, and *lectio divina*, we have his peace and his joy deep within us. We are sheltered in our Home, and we emerge safely, though perhaps a bit battered and wind-torn, on the other side of whatever grief and pain may come our way. When we have neglected these holy habits, however, when we have claimed busyness as a reason for leaving them behind, we are left out on the doorstep to bear the full brunt of the storm. We will eventually still emerge safe in his arms on the other side, but we will carry many more wounds into the rest of our lives.

Pain is inevitable. Our world is broken, and time is broken, and we are broken, and the result of all the brokenness is pain. From loneliness to cancer, from dealing with tantrums to fleeing from hurricanes, we are all suffering.

Jesus did not try to hide this from us. *In this world you will have trouble.*[77] He did not pull a bait-and-switch to convince us that following him would make our lives rosy. In fact, he talks a lot about carrying a cross around as we follow him.[78]

Some of this suffering is chosen. Fasting. Simplicity. Solitude. This kind of holy suffering is what we choose when we decide to practice the spiritual disciplines. Some would go so far as to say that suffering is necessary to living a holy life. It is the way we practice putting to death our sin nature. Jesus' own words seem to bear this out: *If anyone would come after Me, he must deny himself ...*[79] Andrew Murray writes that "Nothing but death, the absolute surrender to death of all that is of nature, will suffice, if the life of God is to be manifested in [us] with power."[80]

This chosen suffering is what creates the space for the Holy Spirit to transform and strengthen our interior world so that we are able to stand up under the pain of the exterior world in order to serve it. An Abba (an older, spiritual mentor) from the 5th century A.D., St. Mark the Ascetic, put it this way: "He who does not choose to suffer for the sake of truth will be chastened more painfully by suffering he has not chosen."[81]

We cannot, of course, trick God into granting us a pain-free life by demonstrating that we have crucified ourselves in advance. Rather, by practicing the killing off of our sin nature through the chosen suffering of self-denial, our spiritual muscles have been strengthened and we are better able to cling to Jesus when suffering comes to us unbidden. It is not, of course, up to us to stand firm amid the storm; God promises to bring us through safely in Christ, regardless of the weakness of our grip. We are, however, saved from much unnecessary suffering when our spiritual muscles are strong enough to keep our eyes fixed on Jesus regardless of the ugly that swirls around us.

Jesus spoke of suffering that is used by God. In the same parable of the vine, he said that *every branch that does bear fruit He prunes, that it may bear more fruit.*[82] Andrew Murray writes that we should be so moved by our abiding in Christ "to hear in each affliction the voice of a messenger that comes to call [us] to abide still more closely. Yes, believer, most specially in times of trial, abide in Christ ... abide in Christ in times of affliction and you shall bring forth more fruit."[83]

James, the brother of Jesus, also speaks of suffering that is used by God. He is so bold as to instruct us to count suffering as pure joy.[84] In the Greek, this word translated *to count* is *hēgeomai*, which means to account as an auditor would. It means that when we are marking our situation down on our life's balance sheet, our times of suffering should be placed in the column marked joy.

What could there be, what could there possibly be in the valley of the deepest dark that could be counted as joy? James does not leave us sinking into despair. He answers with the answer we have been aiming towards from the beginning: our suffering, when we choose to continue to abide in Christ in the middle of it, leads to nothing less than being made perfect and complete. The very *telos* for which we have hoped. It is our choice. We can choose in our pain to more fully make our home in Jesus or to step outside the door.

Whether our suffering is chosen or unwelcomed, the way we choose to respond to suffering matters. Over and over, Scripture tells us that the choices we make in this life ripple forward.[85] What we do with the ebbs and flows in our lives matter. From interruptions to worries, from marriage to loss, every choice we make in response to our circumstances is changing us. Changing the very essence of ourselves into something different from what we are now.[86]

C. S. Lewis said it best. "Taking your life as a whole, with all your innumerable choices, all your life long you are slowly turning this central thing into a heavenly creature or a hellish creature: either into a creature that is in harmony with God, and with other creatures, and with itself, or else into one that is in a state of war and hatred with God, and with its fellow creatures, and with itself."[87]

Choosing to live these holy habits, daily activities like Scripture reading and prayer through *lectio divina*, solitude and silence, are how God the Holy Spirit transforms us into people of his Kingdom. People who, by obedience and love, are helping the Kingdom, God's rule, to break through here and now. People who are at home in Jesus.

Paul speaks all through the book of Philippians of living now as though we were already perfected. One habit leads to another which leads to another which suddenly leads to hope and love breaking through into our world. When we deliberately choose these spiritual disciplines, choose to make the time to be still and know, we slowly become the sort of person who naturally and authentically follows after God. It takes time, it takes choice by painful choice to build these habits, but the more time we put in, the more natural it becomes, and the easier it is to abide when the world is hurling its worst at us.

The poet John Donne shows us how beautiful and natural it can be when we have steeped ourselves in holy habits and are thus able to allow God to transform us through our sufferings rather than to turn away from God in our bitterness or anger. Donne is best known as a great English poet, but he was also a cleric in the Church of England. In 1623, he suffered through a serious illness. So serious, in fact, that he believed he was on his deathbed. During this illness, he wrote *Devotions upon Emergent Occasions*, a book that combines Donne's brilliant writing with his devotion to Christ to illuminate the ways in which we can respond to suffering when we have deliberately given over time in our days to the Holy Spirit.

Donne also wrote of the way God uses suffering to shape us, to mold the dark and dull thing that we are into something extraordinary, something full of light. "Tribulation is treasure in the nature of it, but it is not current money in the use of it, except we get nearer and nearer our home, heaven, by it."[88] Peter Kreeft, in *Heaven: The Heart's Deepest Longing* says something similar: It is "all for our good, the finished product, God's work of art, the Kingdom of Heaven. There is nothing outside heaven except hell. Earth is not outside heaven; it is heaven's workshop, heaven's womb."[89]

The point, after all, of spiritual disciplines, of any spiritual practice, is to allow God to reveal himself to us, to give us himself, to change us into the likeness of himself. This is, remember, our *telos*, our vision of the best life could be. When we are faithful to practice the spiritual disciplines, the Holy Spirit changes us in a way that allows God to fill us with his presence when we are experiencing pain and suffering. This, God's presence, is what we need when we are struck by a sudden storm.

It is what we need, but often it is not what we desire. What we desire is for the storm to vanish, leaving sunshine and rainbows in its wake.

When we are not at home in Christ, we can be blindsided when the storm does not vanish after we have prayed for it to leave us alone. If we are not abiding in God's Word, we can hold false expectations of what God has promised. The storms can harm us much more severely when we are wandering around outside in the cold. When Christ's words are not abiding in us, we can deceive ourselves into believing that we are safe and when the ugly occurs to us or those we love, we are surprised and angry. We strike back at God, even if we claimed unbelief before, putting him on trial for the brokenness we see around us.

Job did the same. When disaster struck, stripping him of material possessions, his children, even his health, he demanded answers from God. "If only I knew where to find him; if only I could go to his dwelling! I would state my case before him and fill my mouth with arguments. I would find out what he would answer me and consider what he would say."[90]

Job demanded explanation, and God responded not by answering his demands but by giving him a guided tour of creation. It seems unsatisfactory. Job wanted to know why his world was burning to ashes around him, and God showed Job the wonders of the zoological world and the stunning beauties of the galaxies and told him, "I created this!" God showed Job the mysteries of our world and our universe and said to him, "I accomplished this!" When Job wanted, even demanded, an answer from God, God gave him something much more beautiful than a simple answer.

God gave Job the same answer that he gives to all who ask, to all who seek: himself. After God had revealed himself to Job through all of his wonders, Job said, "My ears had heard of you but now my eyes have seen you."[91] His seeing, his knowing, came only through great pain.

Is this the only way to know? I don't know the answer to that, yet I do believe that when we choose a holy kind of suffering, a suffering that Jesus also chose, a suffering through the Holy Disciplines, we can know God in a more beautiful and less scarring way.

A brief warning is warranted at this point: the holy habits can also lead to a darkness of their own. We are, after all, in a spiritual war, and

God wants us, in the end, to love him rather than only what comfort he brings to us. Most of our church Fathers and Mothers speak of God veiling himself from them for a season. Sometimes, a long season.

Yet whether our suffering is chosen or unwelcomed, at just the right time, just when we think that we will never find a way out of the darkness and are ready to give up all hope of ever catching a glimpse of light or beauty again, God responds by disclosing, not explanation, but the Light of the world in a deeper way than we have ever seen before.

This is what these holy habits do: they allow the Holy Spirit to change our very hearts so that God can use the ugliness of this world to open us up to receive what is truly the deepest desire of our hearts. Himself.

Cultivating Rhythms

- If you are currently in a season of suffering, have grace with yourself. If you have never practiced these disciplines before, make a beginning, but do not despair. Start small. Do not stop asking God's Spirit to help you abide. The important thing is not that you do the right things and feel successful but that you continue to trust and obey, that you do not give up.

- Find whatever time you can, one minute or one week, and be still with God and with his Word. Practice silence and solitude. Practice *lectio divina* with the passages that hold the most comfort for you. Rest. We are physical beings, and our awareness of God's presence can be directly related to the state of our physical bodies. Do what you can to be healthy.

- Ask the Holy Spirit to show you how to abide in this season and trust that he will stay with you and keep you to the end. Share your grief with God, not in search of quick answers, but simply to tell him about it and allow him to hold it with you and for you. Sometimes merely the act of giving your sorrow to God, of abiding with him in your pain, allows him to help you find the deeper peace that lies beneath.

CHAPTER EIGHT

Seeing God in the Small and the Slow

Pierre Teilhard de Chardin encourages us to *trust in the slow work of God*. This trusting is hard. It is easy to become impatient, to try another, easier way to see God.

CHAPTER EIGHT
Seeing God in the Small and the Slow

For thus said the Lord God, the Holy One of Israel, "... in quietness and in trust shall be your strength."
Isaiah 30:15-18

Yet even once our hearts are open and ready to receive our deepest desire, God himself, often we do not feel as though we have received him. This absence is hard.

All too often we are tempted to think that our problems are too small or insignificant for a big God to trouble with, that we can only see God in the miraculous. We are conditioned to stretch for the large. Instead, he is readily present in the small grace of a quiet hour. The small measure of understanding. The small moment of victory over a sin. We believe that it is a higher godliness to grasp for the more astonishing miracle, the more arduous purity, the more splendid spiritual insight rather than to be thankful for what God has chosen to give.

"We think we dare not be satisfied with the small measure of spiritual knowledge, experience and love that has been given to us, and that we must constantly be looking forward eagerly for the highest good. Then we deplore the fact that we lack the deep certainty, the strong faith, and the rich experience that God has given to others, and we consider this lament to be pious ... Only he who gives thanks for the little things receives the big things."[92]

We miss so many of God's beautiful and perfect gifts when we are focused on the tremendous and the tomorrow instead of looking up and becoming aware of the right now. When God chooses to grant us a small shard of wisdom, a small snatch of victory, a small sliver of intimacy with him, we can know it is enough.

This learning to abide, this making Jesus our home, feels, most of the time, as though nothing is happening. We begin to spend a few minutes most days in silence and solitude. We attempt to practice *lectio divina* through the Lord's Prayer. After a few weeks, we increase our time, if by only a few minutes. Yet nothing happens. Nothing happens during our times of being still; we do not see God. Nothing happens in our lives; we do not become more like God. *Nothing happens.*

I often feel this way. I grow so weary of waiting for God to fulfill His promise to transform me into the image of Jesus: I want to quit fighting my pride and my anger and my jealousy. I want to stop saying the wrong thing to my husband, yelling at my children, hiding from others out of fear. I pray and I try and I pray and I try, and still nothing happens. Or so it seems.

French priest and theologian Pierre Teilhard de Chardin encourages us to *trust in the slow work of God.*

This trusting is hard. It is easy to become impatient, to try another, easier way to see God. Perhaps if we can find the right method to use, the best pattern of words, the correct posture of body ... voila! We will know God. Like magic. Except abiding is not magic. It is a friendship.

We know this, of course. Yet we also do not know this, because we still search for a formula, for exactly the right thing to *do*, rather than simply — being still.

We attempt to control our time with God, both its method and its results, rather than surrendering to God so that he can give us the gift of his presence, the gift of communion with him in whatever form he wishes that to take. This abiding, this making our home in Christ is God's work, so it will always succeed.

Please hear this. I know the heartbreak of submitting to God over and over and feeling as though nothing is happening, as though God is not here, as though we must be doing something horribly wrong. Abiding is God's work, so when we obey, that work will *always* succeed.

When we feel that we have failed at abiding, it is because we have decided what it should look like and then have become frustrated because we cannot make it look that way. Canadian author and teacher David Benner writes that "Prayer is nothing more or less than the interior action of the Trinity at the level of being. This we cannot control; we can only reverently submit."

When it seems that we are not making any progress in bearing fruit, when we still have had no experience of God's presence, when we have been practicing these disciplines of silence and solitude and *lectio divina* for *months* and still feel exactly the same as when we began, know that this is okay. This is normal. This is, in fact, often the way God works. "The Bible shows us that God works through long periods of our lives in which — apparently — nothing much seems to happen."[93]

It is so easy to forget. We forget about Joseph who spent 13 years in slavery before becoming second to Pharaoh. We forget that it took Moses 40 years to get from the burning bush to Canaan. We forget that David waited more than 20 years from the point when Samuel anointed him as king before he actually became king over all of Israel.

Most of us forget that part of fulfilling God's purpose means delay. It takes time to become what God created us to be. Would Joseph or Moses or David have been the leaders they were without the waiting? Would they have been able to live out God's story and lead his people without the process that shaped them into those very leaders? No. And neither can we do anything within God's story without allowing him the time to change our hearts into the beauty he intended.

Whether it takes 13 years or 40, we must accept where we are now, we must be faithful and obedient now, trusting that waiting is not bad, that delay is not ugly. Growing into our role in God's story takes time, so rather than resisting as though it were a setback, let him use that time to make you into who he created you to be. It will be beautiful, I promise.

Remember that God most often works through the small and the slow. "When it comes to doing something about what is wrong in the world, Jesus is best known for his fondness of the minute, the invisible, the quiet, the slow — yeast, salt, seeds, light."[94] This takes time. Andrew

Murray, a pastor in South Africa during the late 19th century, gave this warning: It takes "time to grow into Jesus the Vine: do not expect to abide in Him unless you will give Him that time ... it needs day by day, time with Jesus and with God."[95] In order to abide, we must remain fixed in the place where we are attached to our Vine.

Our transformation into the image of Christ takes time on God's part and it takes time on our part. A magic formula would be easier. We tend to shy away from work, even to become convinced that our relationship with God should not feel like work at all. We hear that our holy transformation depends on the work of the Holy Spirit and are deceived into believing that this means we need not put forth effort. While it is true that there is no amount of work we can do to become more like Christ, we must put in the time needed to give the Holy Spirit space to work. "The measure of sanctification will depend on the measure of abiding in Him."[96]

This kind of transformation takes more than five minutes, twice a week. "Spiritual work is taxing work, and men are loath to do it. Praying, true praying, costs an outlay of serious attention and of time, which flesh and blood do not relish ..."[97] This is enough to discourage us, enough to make us give up all together. We are short on time, pressed for time, out of time for all the tasks we must accomplish in a day. We try to give God more time, then we fail, and we become frustrated and ashamed. We feel guilty and give up, wondering why we even tried in the first place.

Yet the beauty of grace is that we can begin where we are. Start small. God works through the small. Increase the amount of time you spend with God little by little. You will find, as you do, that your desire, your hunger and thirst for God will grow. Not all at once. Not by leaps and bounds, but after a while you will look up from your life and realize that you *want* more time with Him. As you gaze at Jesus through your times of silence and solitude, as you steep yourself in his words, you find that you are drawn to him more and more. You find that you think of him more during the day, that you are more awake to his presence.

It can take months, even years, but one day, you discover that rather than *having* to love those around you, rather than feeling that you *ought* to love those God places in your path, you *want* to love them. "A holy life would not be so rare or so difficult a thing if our devotions were not so short and hurried ... Our ability to stay with God in our closet measures our ability to stay with God out of the closet."[98] Consider those gifts of service that we tried (and failed) to give to God on our own terms, those acts of compassion to others that did not go the way we planned. Once we have been filled with Christ as we learn to abide in him, we receive those gifts and acts back from God. "We receive them back, to hold them as His property, to wait on him for the grace to use them aright day by day, and to have them act only under his influence."[99]

I know I have said it before, but it is so very important that I want to say it again. We who want desperately to hear from God, to know him more, to experience his presence — we must listen closely. Abiding in the vine of Jesus is God's work, so it will always succeed. Always.

Our work is simply to be still. *Be still and know that I am God.*

Do not be discouraged. We are all beginners in this. Even those who have practiced silence and solitude and *lectio divina* for decades still count themselves as beginners. Thomas Merton, a twentieth century monk who had dedicated himself to these habits, wrote, "We do not want to be beginners. But let us be convinced of the fact that we will never be anything else but beginners, all our life!"

Personally, I still feel like a beginner in this. I mostly still feel no change, mostly still struggle to believe that this discipline is working anything good in me at all. Yet I am catching glimpses of growing awareness of God's presence. Even more, I trust in the lives and writings of those who have gone before, those who write of the beauty that results from these practices.

I resonate with David Benner who writes, "Prayer remains a struggle for me. On the other hand, so does forgiving someone who has wronged me. So does loving my neighbor ... I persist because I am fulfilling God's command, and also because I believe I am doing what is best for me whether or not I feel like it at the time." I, too, believe the Scriptures that tell me that this is what God wants me to do. Am I willing to offer these disciplines to Him as a sacrifice, regardless of what I may or may not receive or perceive in practicing them? I believe so. I hope so. I pray that He will give me the grace to do so. I truthfully have little to show for all my practicing of silence and solitude, of *lectio divina*, yet I cannot give up, for *so pants my soul for You, O God.*[100]

Lord, to whom should we go? You have the words of eternal life.[101]

Patient Trust

Above all, trust in the slow work of God.
We are quite naturally impatient in everything
to reach the end without delay.
We should like to skip the intermediate stages.
We are impatient of being on the way to something
unknown, something new.
And yet it is the law of all progress
that it is made by passing through
some stages of instability—
and that it may take a very long time.

And so I think it is with you;
your ideas mature gradually — let them grow,
let them shape themselves, without undue haste.
Don't try to force them on,
as though you could be today what time
(that is to say, grace and circumstances
acting on your own good will)
will make of you tomorrow.

Only God could say what this new spirit
gradually forming within you will be.
Give our Lord the benefit of believing
that his hand is leading you,
and accept the anxiety of feeling yourself
in suspense and incomplete.

—Pierre Teilhard de Chardin

Cultivating Rhythms

- In your times of stillness with God, think over your practices and rhythms so far. Where do you feel satisfied about the way things are going? Where do you feel frustrated? Talk with God about that.

- Spend some time meditating on the slow work of God. Ask the Spirit to help you trust his pace and timing. Ask him to help you let go of the need to control the outcomes of your disciplines and habits.

- Ask the Holy Spirit to show you where you are focused on the tremendous and the tomorrow instead of looking up and becoming aware of the right now. Ask him to change your mindset.

- Practice *lectio divina* (see chapter four) in Jude 1:24-25.

CHAPTER NINE

*Giving God Stillness and Space
to Do His Good Work*

Even the image of the vine to which we keep returning speaks of this work as being God's. Jesus was not capricious with his choice of imagery. Jesus names God as the vinedresser, while we are only branches. In any vineyard, the vinedresser is the one who does the work while the branches simply ... are.

CHAPTER NINE

Giving God Stillness and Space to Do His Good Work

You did not choose me, but I chose you and appointed you that you should go and bear fruit and that your fruit should abide ...
John 15:16

This waiting is hard, at least partly because we want so desperately to *do* something in our life with God. We depend on grace for our redemption and then attempt to depend on ourselves for our sanctification. We are so often taught, even in our churches, that we must put forth effort in order to become more like Christ, that justification is God's work while sanctification is our work, done with the help of the Holy Spirit to be sure, but our work, nonetheless.

"Incalculable harm has been done to the deeper spirituality of the Church, by the idea that when once we are God's children the using of our gifts in His service follows as a matter of course ... I must feel that I cannot at once proceed to use them for God's glory. I must first lay them at Christ's feet, to be accepted and cleansed by Him ... I receive them back, to hold them as His property, to wait on Him for the grace to use them aright day by day, and to have them act only under His influence."[102]

We immediately leap into serving others and then become discouraged when our plans fail. We grow hopeless when gratitude for our salvation, desire to please God, even prayer alone is not enough to change our hearts.

These spiritual disciplines we have been pondering are only practices that put us in the place where the Holy Spirit can do His work. It is true that learning these practices is a difficult task, yet all of these holy habits amount to nothing more than being still before God. We practice being still, practice yielding to the Spirit, yet we can do *nothing* active to change our hearts. The only work we can do is that of putting ourselves in the space where the Spirit brings out fruit in us. Just as Jesus did the work to make us his, so only he can do the work in our hearts to make us truly abide in him.

Brother Lawrence spoke of this when he mentioned his failings at bearing fruit. A friend wrote this of him: "When he had failed in his duty, he only confessed his fault saying to God, 'I shall never do otherwise, if you leave me to myself. It is You who must hinder my failing and mend what is amiss.' Then, after this, he gave himself no further uneasiness about it."[103] I, on the other hand, agonize over my disobedience. When I have failed to abide during a day, when I have failed to think of God even once in a morning, I become discouraged and tempted to give up. I forget that abiding is not my work.

We can do nothing on our own. Sometimes, I admit, this is frustrating. I enjoy being competent, accomplished in my own merit. Most of the time, however, this truth is freeing. We can do nothing apart from Jesus, so we are free to lay down our weapons and let him fight for us. Jesus said we *cannot* bear fruit unless we abide in him, that we can do absolutely nothing apart from him.[104] Where does that leave us? If nothing we do is good enough, if we are destined to fail no matter how hard we try, where in our life-with-God does this leave us?

This leaves us with hope.

We are no longer under the law. We are not held under the command of *you must do* but under the promise of *you will be*. These disciplines of silence and solitude and of *lectio divina* that we have been considering are some of the best ways we have for allowing the Holy Spirit to transform our hearts. Yet they are not commands we must obey.

I want to repeat here an assertion I quoted earlier from Annie Dillard: "Experience has taught the race that if knowledge of God is the end, then these habits of life are not the means but the condition in which the means operate."[105]

This is Jesus's promise. When we abide in him, we will bear much fruit.[106] When God commands us to be holy as he is holy, when he commands us to love him with all of our heart, soul, mind, and strength, when he commands us to love others as we love ourselves, we find that his commands turn out to be a promise.

Frederick Buechner says this: "The final secret, I think, is this: that the words 'You shall love the Lord your God' become, in the end, less a command than a promise. And the promise is that, yes, on the weary feet of faith and the fragile wings of hope, we will come to love him at last as from the first he has loved us — loved us even in the wilderness, especially in the wilderness, because he has been in the wilderness with us. He has been in the wilderness for us." The covenant has been made with God, and we find that God has not only fulfilled his part but our own part as well. *I will put the fear of me in their hearts, that they may not turn from me.*[107]

Even the image of the vine to which we keep returning speaks of this work as being God's. Jesus was not capricious with his choice of imagery. Jesus names God as the vinedresser, while we are only branches. In any vineyard, the vinedresser is the one who does the work while the branches simply ... are.

Paul Jensen, in his book *Subversive Spirituality*, surveys the spirituality and rhythms of three Christian movements: pre-Reformation, Catholic Reformation, and the Protestant Puritan movement. One of the commonalities he found among all three of these was the emphasis of the leaders only to be still and allow God to do the work. Solitude with God always came before mission.

The leaders had built into their lives rhythms of inner spirituality that supported their outward missions. "When outward mission is accompanied by compassion, healing, and transformation, people are drawn, often in crowds, to the missionary. At this point, the mission's greatest danger lies in its potential to consume the missionary with busyness, exhaustion, and prayerlessness, unless adequate inner rhythms are created, protected, and honored. Jesus and other leaders examined in this study felt the need for periodic escape from the crowds with their needs so they could move inward for solitary or communal prayer."[108]

In other words, no matter what the kingdom mission given to you by God, you cannot sustain it without regular rhythms of stillness before God. *You cannot sustain any godly mission on your own.*

It is when we simply are still, keeping our gaze fixed on Christ through such habits as silence and solitude and *lectio divina*, that the Holy Spirit changes us and stirs us to his work. "It is when the soul becomes utterly passive, looking and resting on what Christ is to do, that its energies are stirred to their highest activity, and that we work most effectually because we know that he works in us."[109]

As the Spirit of God dwells in us, we are more and more able to be led by the Spirit to do the work he has for us.[110] We cannot charge ahead and try to take the lead, but rather, must wait on the Spirit to change us, to instruct us, to show us the way in which we should go. It is the Spirit's role within the trinity to produce fruit, to bring every work to completion.

We see this in a beautiful way through the early Church.[111] As we read in the book of Acts, the Holy Spirit leads the Church in her various missions, sending people out as they are waiting on him in prayer. He gives direction and the words to say, he produces the fruit, and the only thing the people do is to follow. The Spirit is the one who gives joy and spreads the Word.

The Holy Spirit does his work as he moves us to do our work. As we are still before God, we learn to understand how the *apart from me you can do nothing* is only the beginning of the *I can do all things through*

Christ who strengthens me.[112] We can finally take a breath and simply rest in him. He will do the work. We must only wait for him.

One thing to remember is that God will give us grace to abide for today. We are not asked to abide for weeks and years at a time, but for today. For this moment. We will abide for weeks and years to come, but in each day during those weeks and years, God will ask us to abide in him today.

When you look up from your work, whatever that work may be, and realize that you have not thought of Jesus for hours on end, rather than despair, simply breathe and tell the Father that you trust him to keep you abiding in him right now. It does not matter whether you *feel* as though you were abiding. Will you trust Jesus to keep you in him for this one moment? "Abide in Him at this present moment. Instead of wasting effort in trying to get into a state that will last, just remember that it is Christ Himself, the living, loving Lord, who alone can keep you, and is waiting to do so."[113]

One last word from Andrew Murray regarding the choice we face: "... one is the carnal way, in which we put forth our utmost efforts and resolutions, trusting Christ to help us in doing so. The other, the spiritual way, in which, as those who have died and can do nothing, our one care is to receive Christ day by day, and at every step to let Him live and work in us."[114] I know which choice sounds more life-giving to me.

Cultivating Rhythms

- Contemplate the idea of this being God's work and not yours. Does this bring you relief? Does it bring you frustration? Speak with God about this, being sure to listen as well.

- Make a list of all the things that you "do for God." Pray over them, allowing the Spirit time to speak to you about your intentions, then submit all your works to God.

- Practice releasing control of your abiding to God. Take three deep breaths. Open your hands and lay them, palm up, in your lap. Ask God to teach you to abide. Listen. Thank him for always being with you. Take three more deep breaths. Go about your day and, regardless of what you feel, trust that he is helping you to abide.

CHAPTER TEN

Conclusion

Coming Home to Stay

Jesus calls us to make him our home so that through us, others can come Home, too.

CHAPTER TEN

Conclusion: Coming Home to Stay

As the Father has loved me, so have I loved you. Abide in my love.

John 15:9

There are things in life which are common to us all. We all have pieces of our lives that are ordinary, common, and mundane. We all have pieces of our lives that bring pain, suffering, and ugliness. We all dream of home. Whether we have experienced a true home or have only read about such things, we all dream of a place where we are loved unconditionally and are safe. We dream of a place of light and warmth, of comfort and contentment. We dream, whether we know it or not, of finding our home in Jesus.

We must be taught how to abide in Christ. We cannot even do this much on our own. We must watch Jesus, imitate his life, do the things he did in order to learn how to abide in him as he abides in the Father. What we call the spiritual disciplines are simply the spiritual activities Jesus practiced while on this earth. When we weave these same habits into our days, we are simply following Jesus. We are following Jesus as he lived out his everyday life and we are following Jesus as he went through the kind of suffering most of us will never know. We are following Jesus as he lived the life of all humanity.

It is this following after Jesus that opens us up to knowing God. These holy habits allow the space in our lives and our hearts for the Holy Spirit to transform us into the people God created us to be, the people who know God and dwell in him ... and look just like him. Our world desperately needs "little Christs,"[115] people who bear much fruit because they are abiding in Jesus.

God created us to know him and love him and to live a life that is full of loving others. This abiding in Christ, this making our home in him, is the way in which we are given the supernatural ability to do this. He who gives the command to love God and love people is the same One who gives the command to abide in him. He who instructs us that the way we love him is to love one another is the same One who instructs us to abide in his love. "Understand that He who gave the command in such close connection with His teaching about the Vine and the abiding in Him, gave us in that the assurance that we have only to abide in Him to be able to love like Him."[116]

Our world, the little piece of the world where we live, is full of people who are drowning in the loneliness of the ordinary. Our world is full of people who are being crushed by the ugliness of pain. Jesus is the light of home that shines out, drawing us into himself. He calls us, his disciples, to be the people who abide, the people who reflect his light to the bit of world in which He placed us. Jesus calls us to make him our home so that through us, others can come Home, too.

And now, little children, abide in Him, so that when He appears we may have confidence and not shrink from Him in shame at His coming.[117]

Now to him who is able to keep you from stumbling and to present you blameless before the presence of his glory with great joy, to the only God, our Savior, through Jesus Christ our Lord, be glory, majesty, dominion, and authority, before all time and now and forever. Amen.[118]

FURTHER RESOURCES

For the practices of silence and solitude, *lectio divina*, and retreating, explore the writings of Ruth Haley Barton (*Invitation to Solitude and Silence* and *Invitation to Retreat*), David Benner (*Opening to God: Lectio Divina and Life as Prayer*), and Emilie Griffin (*Wilderness Time: A Guide to Spiritual Retreat*). The *Pray As You Go* app is also a good tool for many of the disciplines mentioned in this book.

For more on abiding in Christ, read Andrew Murray's little book, *Abide in Christ*.

For all other authors quoted in this book, see the bibliography provided at the end of this book.

ENDNOTES

Chapter One

[1] John 15:4

[2] Some of the thoughts about this imagery were found in the *Dictionary of Biblical Imagery,* p. 916-17

[3] Matthew 26:27-28

[4] John 15

[5] *The Pursuit of God*, p. 15

[6] I Chronicles 29:15

[7] I Peter 2:11

[8] Matthew 28:20

[9] John 15:11

[10] Andrew Murray in *Abide in Christ*, p. 8-9

Chapter Two

[11] Exodus 19:5-6, Romans 8, I Peter 2:9, and Revelation 5:9-10, as examples

[12] Jeremy Begbie in *Resounding Truth*

[13] Jeremy Begbie in *Resounding Truth*

[14] II Peter 1:4

[15] *The Meaning of Reality*, p. 10

[16] Annie Dillard, *Teaching a Stone to Talk*, p. 64

[17] *The Life of Antony and the Letter to Marcinellus*, p. 23

[18] Hosea 6:6

[19] Jeremiah 9:23

[20] Psalm 46:10

[21] Andrew Murray in *Abide in Christ*, p. 78

[22] Isaiah 30:15

[23] Madeleine L'Engle in *Walking on Water*, p. 218

[24] Ruth Haley Barton in *Invitation to Solitude and Silence*, p. 73

[25] David Benner in *Opening to God*, p. 289

Chapter Three

[26] David Benner in *Opening to God,* p. 49

[27] *Opening to God*, p. 164

[28] Matthew 11:28

[29] Exodus 19, 24, 34

[30] Daniel 6

[31] Psalm 42:1

[32] Acts 1

[33] Luke 5:16, 6:12-13, Mark 1:35, 6:46, among others

[34] *The Life of Moses*

[35] Marcelle Auclair in *Saint Teresa of Avila*, p. 155

[36] *Power Through Prayer,* p.90

[37] *The Way of the Heart: The Spirituality of the Desert Fathers and Mothers*, p. 171, 201

[38] *Invitation to Solitude and Silence*, p. 128-129

[39] *The Silent Life,* p. 167

[40] *The Orthodox Way,* p. 52

[41] *The Way of the Heart,* p. 227

Chapter Four

[42] John 1:1

[43] *Life with God,* p. 62

[44] Dallas Willard, a theologian and philosopher who comes from the Southern Baptist tradition, in *Hearing God*, p. 163-164

[45] Eugene Peterson, pastor and theologian known for his Message Bible translation, in *Eat This Book,* p. 116

[46] Joshua 1:8

[47] Psalm 119:15

[48] Psalm 119:148

[49] Psalm 143:5

[50] *The Orthodox Way,* p.111

[51] *The Orthodox Way,* p. 111
[52] Isaiah 6:1-8
[53] *Eat This Book,* p. 55

Chapter Five
[54] *Subversive Spirituality*
[55] *Daring Greatly,* p. 144
[56] *Daring Greatly,* p. 145
[57] *The Search for Compassion,* p. 12
[58] Romans 5:5
[59] *The Search for Compassion,* p. 94-95
[60] *Subversive Spirituality*
[61] Deuteronomy 6:4-7

Chapter Six
[62] Colossians 1:16-17
[63] I Corinthians 10:31
[64] John 5:19
[65] p. 102
[66] *Abide in Christ,* p. 102
[67] *The Pursuit of God,* p.62
[68] p. 32
[69] John 15
[70] Andrew Murray in *Abide in Christ,* p. 98
[71] p. 26
[72] *Practicing the Presence of God,* p. 5-6
[73] p. 24
[73] *Listening to Your Life,* p. 87

Chapter Seven

[75] John 16:33

[76] John 16:33, II Thessalonians 3:16, II Corinthians 7:4, Galatians 5:22, among many others

[77] John 16:33

[78] Luke 9:23

[79] Luke 9:23

[80] *Abide in Christ,* p. 121

[81] in *On the Spiritual Law,* p. 123

[82] John 15:2

[83] *Abide in Christ,* p. 80, 82

[84] James 1:2

[85] Matthew 25:31-46, for example

[86] Romans 5:3-5

[87] in *Mere Christianity,* p. 92

[88] *Devotions upon Emergent Occasions,* p. 58

[89] p. 108-109

[90] Job 23:3-5 NIV

[91] Job 42:5

Chapter Eight

[92] Dietrich Bonhoeffer in *Life Together*

[93] Richard Foster in *Life with God,* p. 125

[94] Eugene Peterson in *Tell It Slant,* p. 70

[95] *Abide in Christ,* p. 4

[96] Andrew Murray in *Abiding in Christ,* p. 40

[97] E. M. Bounds in *Power Through Prayer,* p. 88

[98] *Power Through Prayer,* p. 90

[99] *Abiding in Christ,* p. 70

[100] Psalm 42:1

[101] John 6:68

Chapter Nine

[102] Andrew Murray in *Abide in Christ,* p. 69-70

[103] *The Practice of the Presence of God*

[104] John 15:4-5

[105] *Teaching a Stone to Talk*

[106] John 15:5

[107] Jeremiah 32:40

[108] *Subversive Spirituality*

[109] Andrew Murray in *Abide in Christ,* p. 15

[110] Romans 8:5-11

[111] Acts 13

[112] *Abide in Christ,* p. 97

[113] *Abide in Christ,* p. 65

[114] *Abide in Christ,* p. 124

Chapter Ten

[115] C. S. Lewis in *Mere Christianity,* p. 177

[116] *Abide in Christ,* p. 110

[117] I John 2:28

[118] Jude 1:24-25

BIBLIOGRAPHY

Athanasius. (1980). *The Life of Antony and the Letter to Marcellinus.* Mahwah, NJ: Paulist Press.

Auclair, Marcelle. (1988). *Saint Teresa of Avila.* Petersham, MA: St. Bede's Publications.

Barton, Ruth Haley. (2004). *Invitation to Solitude and Silence.* Downers Grove, IL: InterVarsity Press.

Benner, David. (2010). *Opening to God: Lectio Divina and Life as Prayer.* Downers Grove, IL: InterVarsity Press.

Bounds, E.M. (2013). *Power Through Prayer.* Seaside, OR: Rough Draft Printing.

Brother Lawrence. (1977). *Practicing the Presence of God.* New York, NY: Doubleday.

Buechner, Frederick. (1991). *Listening to Your Life: Daily Meditations with Frederick Buechner.* New York, NY: HarperCollins Publishers.

Dillard, Annie. (1982). *Teaching a Stone to Talk: Expeditions and Encounters.* New York, NY: HarperCollins Publishers.

Donne, John. (1999). *Devotions upon Emergent Occasions and Death's Duel.* New York: Random House, Inc.

Foster, Richard J. (2008). *Life with God.* New York, NY: HarperOne.

Gregory of Nyssa. (1978). *The Life of Moses.* Mahwah, NJ: Paulist Press.

Jenson, L. Paul. (2009). *Subversive Spirituality: Transforming Mission through the Collapse of Space and Time.* Eugene, OR: Pickwick Publications.

Kreeft, Peter J. (1980). *Heaven: The Heart's Deepest Longing.* San Francisco: Harper & Row.

L'Engle, Madeleine. (1972). *Walking on Water: Reflections on Faith and Art.* Colorado Springs, CO: Waterbrook Press.

Lewis, C. S. (2001). *Mere Christianity.* New York: HarperCollins.

Merton, Thomas. (1957). *The Silent Life.* Wilmington, MA: Mariner Books.

Murray, Andrew. (2019). *Abide in Christ.* Lexington, KY: Andrew Murray Books.

Nouwen, Henri. (1994). *The Way of the Heart: The Spirituality of the Desert Fathers and Mothers.* New York, NY: HarperCollins Publishers.

Peterson, Eugene H. (2006). *Eat This Book: A Conversation in the Art of Spiritual Reading.* Grand Rapids, MI: William B. Eerdmans Publishing Company.

Purves, Andrew. (1989). *The Search for Compassion: Spirituality and Ministry.* Louisville, KY: Westminster/John Knox Press

Ryken, Leland, Wilhoit, James C., & Longman III, Tremper (Eds.). Vine, Vineyard. In *Dictionary of Biblical Imagery.* (pp. 914-917). Downers Grove, IL: InterVarsity Press.

St. Mark the Ascetic. (1983). "On the Spiritual Law," in The Philokalia, vol. 1, ed. G. E. H.

Palmer, Philip Gherrard and Kallistos Ware. London: Faber and Faber.

Tozer, A. W. (2016). *The Pursuit of God.* Middletown, DE: Mockingbird Classics Publishing.

Ware, Bishop Kallistos. (1979). *The Orthodox Way.* Crestwood, NY: St Vladimir's Seminary Press.

Yannaras, Christos. (2011). *The Meaning of Reality.* Alhambra, CA: Sebastian Press.

AUTHOR

Elizabeth is both writer and musician, who practices her writing craft weekly at her blog, MadeSacred.com, and practices her musical craft at church and while teaching piano lessons. She earned undergraduate and master's degrees in music education, and she holds a Certificate of Spiritual Formation from Lincoln Christian University. Elizabeth also loves the visual beauty of life, including photography and art, and enjoys weaving words with art on her blog to create something new. She is a wife to her logical, programmer husband, a homeschooling mother to four intense, warrior girls, and a Midwestern girl who loves the sight of golden fields stretching to the horizon. She neglects housework in favor of reading as many books as she can get her hands on and loves to travel the world. You can connect with her at MadeSacred.com, on Facebook as @MadeSacred, and on Instagram as @ElizabethGiger.

Made in the USA
Las Vegas, NV
09 February 2021